RODRIGO

The Girl
Who Became a Star

This book belongs to

_____

CONTENTS

CHAPTER 1

Early Years

In the sunny city of Murrieta, California, a little girl named Olivia Isabel Rodrigo was born on February 20, 2003. She came into the world as the only child of Jennifer, a school teacher, and Chris, a family therapist. From the very beginning, Olivia's life was filled with love, laughter, and music.

Growing up in the nearby town of Temecula, Olivia discovered her passion for performing at a young age. Despite being born half-deaf in her left ear, she never let anything hold her back. With the support of her family, Olivia embraced her uniqueness and embarked on a journey to share her talent with the world.

Early Years

In the sunny city of Murrieta, California, a little girl named Olivia Isabel Rodrigo was born on February 20, 2003. She came into the world as the only child of Jennifer, a school teacher, and Chris, a family therapist. From the very beginning, Olivia's life was filled with love, laughter, and music.

Growing up in the nearby town of Temecula, Olivia discovered her passion for performing at a young age. Despite being born half-deaf in her left ear, she never let anything hold her back. With the support of her family, Olivia embraced her uniqueness and embarked on a journey to share her talent with the world.

Olivia comes from a diverse background. While she is Filipino American, her mother has German and Irish ancestry. Olivia takes pride in her Filipino heritage, embracing traditions and cuisine passed down through generations. She fondly recalls growing up surrounded by the vibrant sounds of alternative rock music, inspired by her parents' favorite bands like No Doubt, Pearl Jam, the White Stripes, and Green Day.

As Olivia's love for music continued to grow, so did her desire to share her talent with others. Little did she know, her journey was just beginning, and the world was about to discover the incredible young talent that would one day become a household name.

As a young girl, Olivia Rodrigo's love for performing blossomed at Lisa J. Mails Elementary School in Murrieta. She eagerly participated in the after-school musical theater program, where she discovered the magic of being on stage and bringing characters to life through music and acting.

At the tender age of five, Olivia's parents recognized her talent and enrolled her in vocal lessons with Jennifer Dustman. These lessons helped Olivia explore her vocal range and hone her singing skills. Encouraged by Dustman, Olivia also began entering local singing competitions, where she dazzled audiences with her talent and passion for music.

At the age of nine, Olivia started taking piano lessons. With determination and passion, she immersed herself in learning this new instrument, eager to expand her musical horizons.

Inspired by the heartfelt songs of country music superstar Taylor Swift, Olivia's interest in songwriting began to blossom. She picked up the guitar at the age of 12 and soon found herself pouring her heart into creating her own music, drawing from her own experiences and emotions.

Acting Adventures Begin

In 2010, at the age of seven, Olivia had her first taste of on-screen acting, appearing in an Old Navy commercial. But it was in 2015, at the age of twelve, Olivia Rodrigo took the entertainment world by storm with her acting debut in the direct-to-video film "An American Girl: Grace Stirs Up Success." Portraying the lead role of Grace Thomas, Olivia captured hearts with her charm and talent, leaving audiences wanting more.

Despite her budding success in acting, Olivia remained focused on her education. She attended Dorothy McElhinney Middle School in Murrieta for a year before embarking on a new chapter in her life.

In 2016, Olivia's dreams took her to Los Angeles after landing a role in Disney Channel's "Bizaardvark." Despite the move, Olivia continued her education through homeschooling, balancing her studies with her burgeoning career in acting and music.

In the world of "Bizaardvark," Olivia's star continued to rise as she portrayed the character Paige Olvera, a talented guitarist with a flair for comedy. Audiences quickly fell in love with Olivia's infectious energy and magnetic presence, making her a fan favorite for three thrilling seasons.

But Olivia's journey was far from over. In February 2019, she landed the starring role of Nini Salazar-Roberts in the Disney+ series "High School Musical: The Musical: The Series." Premiering later that year, the show showcased Olivia's acting prowess and musical talents, earning her praise from fans and critics alike.

Not content with just acting, Olivia also wrote and performed the promotional single "All I Want" for the series, showcasing her skills as a singer-songwriter. As the series progressed, Olivia's star continued to shine brightly. But in a bold move, she made the decision to leave the show at the end of its third season to focus on her music career. It was a decision that would set her on a path to even greater success, as the world would soon come to discover.

CHAPTER 3

Sour: A Sweet Success

In 2020, Olivia Rodrigo took a monumental step in her career by signing with Geffen Records. But what made this record deal truly special was that Olivia negotiated to retain ownership of the masters of her music, empowering herself as an artist.

On January 8, 2021, Olivia released her debut single, "Drivers License," which she co-wrote with producer Dan Nigro. The song immediately captured the hearts of listeners around the world, receiving critical acclaim and breaking records left and right.

Within just a week of its release, "Drivers License" made history on Spotify, breaking the record twice for most daily streams ever for a non-holiday song. With over 15.7 million global streams on January 11 and over 17 million global streams the next day, the song skyrocketed to the top of the charts, becoming an instant sensation.

But the success didn't stop there. "Drivers License" went on to break yet another Spotify record as the first song in history to hit 80 million streams in just 7 days. It debuted at number one on the Billboard Hot 100 chart and reached the top spot in numerous other countries around the world.

For Olivia, the whirlwind success of "Drivers License" was both thrilling and surreal. In an interview, she reflected on the experience, mentioning that it had been the absolute craziest week of her life and that her entire life had shifted in an instant. It was a moment she would never forget, marking the beginning of a new chapter in her already remarkable journey.

On April 1, 2021, Olivia Rodrigo released her follow-up single, "Deja Vu," and once again, she made history. The song debuted at number eight on the Billboard Hot 100, making Olivia the first artist to debut their first two releases in the top 10 of the Hot 100. It was a remarkable achievement for the young star, solidifying her place as a rising talent in the music industry.

Just over a month later, Olivia released the third single preceding her debut album, "Good 4 U," on May 14, 2021. The song soared to the top of the charts, becoming her second single to debut at number one on the Hot 100. Fans couldn't get enough of Olivia's music, eagerly awaiting the release of her debut studio album.

And on May 21, 2021, their patience was rewarded when Olivia's debut album, "Sour," hit the shelves. The album was met with critical acclaim, with Slate's Chris Molanphy praising its first three singles for establishing Olivia's "early status as Gen-Z's most versatile new artist." Critics and fans alike hailed Olivia as one of Generation Z's finest artists, with Variety even dubbing her "the voice of her generation" in a cover story.

"Sour" made its mark on the charts as well, debuting at number one on the Billboard 200 chart and spending a total of five weeks at the top spot. Olivia's album became the longest reigning number-one album by a female artist in 2021, solidifying her status as a force to be reckoned with in the music industry.

With "Sour," Olivia proved that she was more than just a one-hit wonder, establishing herself as a powerhouse performer and a true musical talent.

CHAPTER 4

Reaching New Heights

In June 2021, Olivia Rodrigo treated fans to an unforgettable experience with the premiere of "Sour Prom," a prom-themed concert film on YouTube.

Just three days later, Olivia received a remarkable honor when Time magazine named her Entertainer of the Year. It was a testament to Olivia's talent and the impact she had made on the entertainment industry in such a short time.

In December 2021, Olivia delighted fans once again with a special Christmas surprise. She shared a snippet of a Christmas song called "The Bels," which she had written and recorded at the young age of five. It was a heartwarming reminder of Olivia's passion for music, which has been with her since childhood.

As the year came to a close, Olivia's achievements continued to pile up. According to Billboard, she closed out 2021 as the bestselling singles artist worldwide, with eight songs on the year-end Global 200 chart. "Drivers License," "Good 4 U," and "Deja Vu" were among the top-ranked songs, showcasing Olivia's undeniable impact on the music industry.

"Sour" was also a massive success, ranking as the third bestselling album of 2021 in the US and the fourth bestselling album in the UK. Both the album and Olivia's breakout hit, "Drivers License," were Spotify's most streamed album and song globally, further cementing Olivia's status as a global superstar.

The International Federation of the Phonographic Industry (IFPI) recognized Olivia as the tenth bestselling artist of 2021, with "Sour" ranking as the second bestselling album of the year.

To celebrate the success of "Sour," Olivia embarked on her debut headlining tour, the Sour Tour, which took her across the United States, Canada, and Europe from April to July 2022. It was a triumphant journey for Olivia, as she continued to shine brightly on stages around the world, captivating audiences with her voice and infectious energy.

But the excitement didn't stop there. Olivia's talent and hard work were recognized once again when she received seven nominations at the 64th Annual Grammy Awards. Among the nominations were prestigious categories like Best New Artist, Album of the Year for "Sour," and Record of the Year and Song of the Year for "Drivers License."

Olivia's incredible achievements were celebrated at the Grammy Awards ceremony, where she took home three awards. She won the coveted title of Best New Artist, along with Best Pop Vocal Album for "Sour" and Best Pop Solo Performance for "Drivers License." It was a night of triumph and celebration for Olivia, as she stood on stage, proudly clutching her well-deserved awards.

On March 25, 2022, Olivia Rodrigo's journey reached another milestone with the release of her Disney+ documentary film, "Olivia Rodrigo: Driving Home 2 U." The documentary offered fans a behind-the-scenes look at the making of her debut album, "Sour," giving them a glimpse into Olivia's creative process and the stories behind the music.

In 2022, while crafting new music for her next album, Olivia attended a poetry class at the University of Southern California. During the class, Olivia found herself drawn to one of her homework pieces, which she would later repurpose into the song "Lacy." This heartfelt song would go on to appear on the tracklist of her upcoming album, showcasing her ability to draw inspiration from the world around her.

On March 25, 2022, Olivia Rodrigo's journey reached another milestone with the release of her Disney+ documentary film, "Olivia Rodrigo: Driving Home 2 U." The documentary offered fans a behind-the-scenes look at the making of her debut album, "Sour," giving them a glimpse into Olivia's creative process and the stories behind the music.

In 2022, while crafting new music for her next album, Olivia attended a poetry class at the University of Southern California. During the class, Olivia found herself drawn to one of her homework pieces, which she would later repurpose into the song "Lacy." This heartfelt song would go on to appear on the tracklist of her upcoming album, showcasing her ability to draw inspiration from the world around her.

Guts: Embracing Growth

In 2023, Olivia Rodrigo embarked on a new chapter in her musical journey with the release of her second album, "Guts." On September 8, 2023, the world was treated to Olivia's latest masterpiece, which debuted atop the Billboard 200 chart, marking another incredible achievement for the young star.

But even before the release of "Guts," Olivia was already making history. On August 16, 2023, she became the youngest artist to receive the prestigious BRIT Billion Award for achieving over one billion digital streams in the United Kingdom. It was a remarkable honor, cementing Olivia's reputation as a global music phenomenon.

"Guts" was more than just an album for Olivia; it was a journey of self-discovery and growth. Olivia described the album as being about "growing pains," reflecting on the challenges and triumphs of navigating life as a young adult. She felt that she had grown "ten years" between the ages of 18 and 20, and "Guts" was her way of sharing that journey with the world.

The album received widespread critical acclaim from various outlets, with BBC News even declaring it the most critically acclaimed album of 2023. Critics and fans alike praised Olivia for her honesty, vulnerability, and musical prowess, applauding her for creating a body of work that resonated with listeners on a deeply personal level.

The lead single from "Guts," titled "Vampire," was released on June 30 and quickly soared to the top of the charts. It became Olivia's third single to debut atop the Billboard Hot 100, making her the first artist ever to achieve this feat. The album's second single, "Bad Idea Right?," followed suit, reaching the top 10 in both the US and UK, further solidifying Olivia's status as a powerhouse performer and a great musical talent.

In support of her album "Guts," Olivia Rodrigo set off on her second headlining tour, the Guts World Tour. From February to August 2024, Olivia will travel across North America, the UK, and Europe, bringing her music to fans around the world.

But Olivia had even more surprises in store for her fans. On March 20, 2024, she announced that she would release a deluxe version of "Guts" with five additional songs, including the four secret tracks from the vinyl variants. The deluxe edition, titled "Guts (Spilled)," was released on March 22, 2024, giving fans even more music to enjoy and cherish.

With "Guts," Olivia Rodrigo once again proved that she was a force to be reckoned with in the music industry. Her ability to channel her experiences and emotions into powerful, relatable music continued to captivate audiences around the world, leaving them eagerly awaiting her next musical masterpiece.

Inside Olivia's Music

Olivia Rodrigo's journey in music has been shaped by a diverse array of influences and inspirations. From a young age, Olivia looked up to artists like Taylor Swift and Lorde, considering them her idols and primary musical inspirations. In fact, Olivia proudly dubbed herself as Taylor Swift's biggest fan "in the whole world," showcasing her admiration and respect for the superstar.

As Olivia's own musical career blossomed, she continued to pay homage to her influences. In her song "1 Step Forward, 3 Steps Back," Olivia gave interpolation credits to Swift and Jack Antonoff, recognizing their impact on her music. She also retroactively credited Swift, Antonoff, and Annie Clark on her song "Deja Vu," showing her appreciation for their contributions to her artistic journey.

Olivia Rodrigo's success as a songwriter and singer has been guided by her unique voice and heartfelt lyrics. With a voice type classified as soprano, Olivia's vocals soar with emotion and sincerity, captivating listeners with every note.

Despite her rising fame, Olivia remains focused on her passion for songwriting. She has expressed a desire to be known as a songwriter above all else, prioritizing the craft of creating meaningful and authentic music. When choosing to sign with Interscope/Geffen Records, Olivia was drawn to CEO John Janick's praise of her songwriting abilities, rather than her potential as a pop star.

Olivia's songs delve into themes of heartache, mental health, and sadness, offering listeners a glimpse into her own experiences and emotions. Her music resonates with authenticity, presenting realistic perspectives on life and love without veering into melodrama.

As Olivia continues to share her music with the world, she remains committed to crafting songs that speak to the hearts and souls of her listeners. With each new song, Olivia invites audiences to join her on a journey of self-discovery and reflection, proving that the power of music lies in its ability to touch the lives of others in profound and meaningful ways.

Making a Difference

Olivia Rodrigo isn't just a talented musician—she's also a passionate advocate for kindness, equality, and giving back to her community. From encouraging positivity on social media to supporting charitable organizations, Olivia has used her platform to make a positive impact on the world around her.

In partnership with her "Bizaardvark" co-star Madison Hu, Olivia joined forces with Instagram's #KindComments initiative from 2017 to 2018. Together, they encouraged their fans to spread kindness and positivity online, fostering a supportive and uplifting online community.

Olivia's commitment to helping those in need was further demonstrated when she teamed up with the non-profit organization My Friend's Place for their 30th anniversary. Together with Madison Hu, Olivia helped raise over $740,000 for homeless youth, providing them with shelter, food, education, and healthcare.

Throughout her career, Olivia has continued to use her platform to support important causes. She has been an outspoken advocate for gender equality in media, participating as a speaker and panelist for the Geena Davis Institute on Gender in Media.

In 2021, Olivia launched her own merchandise line, "Spicy Pisces T-shirts," with all proceeds benefiting the non-governmental organization "She's the First", which sponsors young girls' scholarship and education.

In 2022, she donated a portion of her tour proceeds to Women for Women International, supporting female survivors of war.

In response to the COVID-19 pandemic, Olivia joined the White House effort to promote vaccinations among young people in the U.S. She met with President Joe Biden and other officials to discuss the importance of vaccination and recorded videos encouraging young people to get vaccinated.

On October 9, 2023, Olivia Rodrigo took to the stage in a special concert at the Los Angeles Theater at Ace Hotel. She performed songs from her album "Guts" in an exclusive event where all proceeds from ticket sales went to her Fund 4 Good nonprofit organization. It was a night filled with music, laughter, and giving back, as Olivia used her platform to make a positive impact in the world.

From spreading kindness online to supporting important causes, Olivia Rodrigo has proven herself to be a true role model and a force for good in the world. As she continues her musical journey, Olivia remains committed to making a positive impact and inspiring others to do the same.

CHAPTER 8

Olivia's Lasting Legacy

Throughout her meteoric rise to fame, Olivia Rodrigo has not only captured the hearts of fans around the world but has also left an indelible mark on the music industry and beyond. Her impact and influence extend far beyond the charts, resonating deeply with young people everywhere.

Olivia's authentic and vulnerable songwriting has struck a chord with listeners of all ages, but particularly with her peers. Through her music, she has fearlessly explored themes of love, heartbreak, and self-discovery, providing a voice for a generation navigating the complexities of adolescence and young adulthood.

But Olivia's influence goes beyond her music alone. As a role model and advocate for positivity and kindness, she has used her platform to inspire young people to be their authentic selves and to spread love and compassion in the world. Olivia has shown that small acts of kindness can make a big difference.

In the ever-evolving landscape of the music industry, Olivia has emerged as a trailblazer, breaking barriers and challenging norms. Her success has paved the way for other young artists to follow their dreams and speak their truth, proving that age is no barrier to achieving greatness.

As Olivia's journey continues, her impact and influence will only continue to grow. With each new song, each new performance, and each new endeavor, she inspires countless young people to chase their dreams, embrace their passions, and make their voices heard.

In the end, Olivia Rodrigo's legacy will not be measured by awards or chart positions, but by the lives she has touched and the hearts she has uplifted. And as her story continues to unfold, one thing is certain: Olivia Rodrigo will always be remembered as more than just a talented musician; she will be remembered as a beacon of hope, empowerment, and positivity for generations to come.

THE END

Made in the USA
Coppell, TX
27 February 2025

46499350R00046